YOSEMITE
NATIONAL PARK

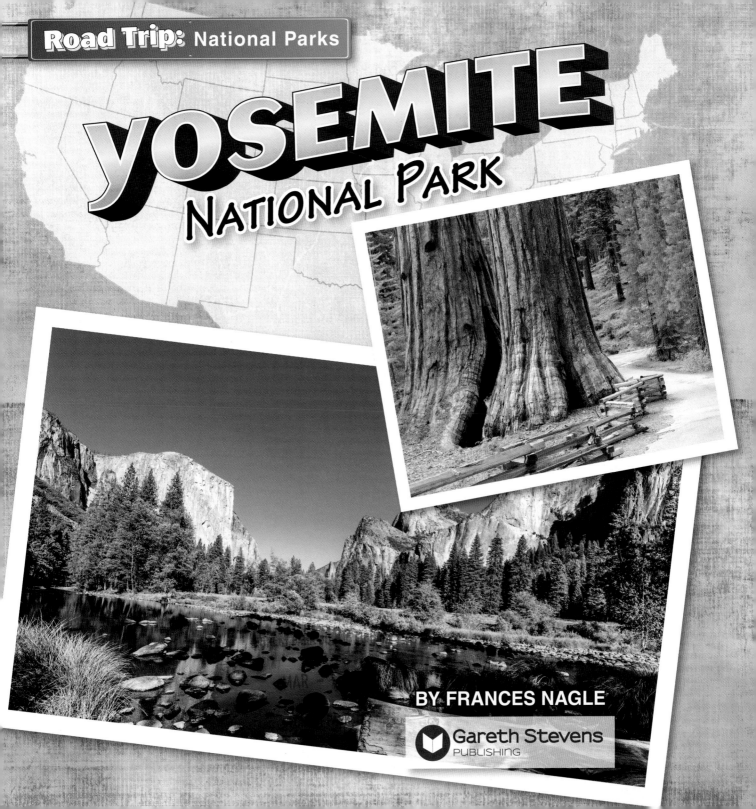

BY FRANCES NAGLE

Gareth Stevens
PUBLISHING

Please visit our website, www.garethstevens.com. For a free color catalog of all our high-quality books, call toll free 1-800-542-2595 or fax 1-877-542-2596.

Library of Congress Cataloging-in-Publication Data

Nagle, Frances.
  Yosemite National Park / Frances Nagle.
      pages cm. — (Road trip: National Parks)
  Includes index.
  ISBN 978-1-4824-1695-4 (pbk.)
  ISBN 978-1-4824-1696-1 (6 pack)
  ISBN 978-1-4824-1694-7 (library binding)
  1. Yosemite National Park (Calif.)—Juvenile literature. I. Title.
  F868.Y6N35 2014
  979.4'47—dc23

                                   2014031947

First Edition

Published in 2016 by
Gareth Stevens Publishing
111 East 14th Street, Suite 349
New York, NY 10003

Designer: Andrea Davison-Bartolotta and Laura Bowen
Editor: Kristen Rajczak

Photo credits: cover, back cover, interior (background texture) Marilyn Volan/Shutterstock.com; cover, p. 1 (right) topseller/Shutterstock.com; cover, p. 1 (left) Mikhail Kolesnikov/Shutterstock.com; pp. 4–20 (blue sign) Vitezslav Valka/ Shutterstock.com; pp. 4–21 (road) Renata Novackova/Shutterstock.com; p. 4 Planet Observer/Universal Images Group/ Getty Images; p. 5 col/Shutterstock.com; p. 7 turtix/Shutterstock.com; p. 9 Roger Viollet/Getty Images; pp. 10, 13 Robert Bohrer/Shutterstock.com; p. 11 (trees) Hanze/Shutterstock.com; pp. 11 (inset), 21 (map) Globe Turner, LLC/ Getty Images; p. 12 C.M.Corcoran/Shutterstock.com; p. 14 Nadia M.B. Hughes/National Geographic/Getty Images; p. 15 (main) Anastasia Tveretinova/Shutterstock.com; p. 15 (inset) Carl Dawson/Shutterstock.com; p. 16 Dmitri Ogleznev/Shutterstock.com; p. 17 Peggy Sells/Shutterstock.com; p. 19 Lorcel/Shutterstock.com; p. 20 (mountains) Sierralara/Shutterstock.com; p. 20 (skier) Chris Falkenstein/Photodisc/Getty Images; p. 21 (notebook) 89studio/ Shutterstock.com.

Printed in the United States of America

CPSIA compliance information: Batch #CS16GS: For further information contact Gareth Stevens, New York, New York at 1-800-542-2595.

Contents

Words in the glossary appear in **bold** type the first time they are used in the text.

Travel to Yosemite

In 1868, **conservationist** John Muir wrote about Yosemite (yoh-SEH-muh-tee) in a letter to a friend: "It is by far the grandest of all the special temples of nature I was ever permitted to enter." Known for its beauty, Yosemite National Park was established largely due to Muir's efforts.

Located in central California, Yosemite National Park is about 140 miles (225 km) from San Francisco and 100 miles (161 km) from the California capital of Sacramento. The park would be a great addition to a road trip on the West Coast!

Yosemite National Park

Sacramento

San Francisco

California

All About
Yosemite National Park

where found: California

year established: 1890 (state park founded in 1864)

size: 1,189 square miles (3,080 sq km)

number of visitors yearly: more than 3 million

common wildlife: black bears, bighorn sheep, western meadowlarks, western pond turtles

common plant life: wildflowers, giant sequoias, hemlocks, pines

major attractions: Yosemite Valley, Yosemite Falls, Pacific Crest National Scenic Trail

Yosemite National Park is one of the most visited parks in the United States.

Pit Stop

Yosemite National Park is found in the Sierra Nevada, a mountain range that runs along the eastern border of California.

Carved by Glaciers

Yosemite National Park has rocky cliffs, steep mountains, and other cool **topography** formed by glaciers slowly moving over the area millions of years ago. Much of the rock in the park is granite, and it's very smooth in some places.

About 2 or 3 million years ago, more glaciers formed over the Sierra Nevada. This knocked rocks loose and carved even more of the present landscape of the park. Rock fall still happens today, meaning Yosemite's topography is always changing.

Pit Stop

There are still glaciers in Yosemite! The Maclure Glacier continues to move slowly downhill, about 1 inch (2.5 cm) every day.

Post

Great **domes** of granite can be found in the park. These mountain forms—such as Half Dome, shown here—are worth seeing in person!

People of Yosemite

The land that would become Yosemite National Park was unknown to white settlers until the 1850s. Until then, only the Ahwahneechee occupied a valley they called Ahwahnee. This Native American people had been there for thousands of years. Then, in 1851, soldiers drove them out.

Others who came to the valley found it so beautiful, they brought photographers and artists in to capture it. They hoped the images would bring in **tourists**. However, traveling over the mountains was hard, so few came at first.

Pit Stop

More visitors came to the area once the Yosemite Valley Railroad was built in the early 1900s.

8

One of the soldiers named the valley "Yosemite." He didn't know it meant "those who kill" and was a name other tribes had for those living in Ahwahnee.

One Big Park

As people came to Yosemite Valley, some became worried about harm to the **environment** there. To **preserve** the scenery, it became a state park in 1864. Roads to the park were added, and about 3,000 people started to visit it each year.

John Muir began campaigning for the US government to **protect** more land in the area. In 1890, Congress made the area around Yosemite State Park a national park. The parks were united as one big national park in 1906.

Devils Postpile

Pit Stop

You can add other nearby protected lands to your road trip to Yosemite, such as Devils Postpile National Monument and Kings Canyon National Park.

More land has been added to Yosemite National Park over the years to bring it to its present size.

Elevation Situation

The park's location in the Sierra Nevada means there are great **elevation** differences throughout it. This has created many different **habitats**. There are lakes in the valleys and meadows that bloom with wildflowers in the summer. Forests are full of gray foxes, spotted owls, and many kinds of bats.

The higher you go in the park, the fewer plants and animals there are. At about 6,000 feet (1,830 m), you'll find red fir, juniper, and lodgepole pine trees.

spotted owl

Pit Stop

Two rivers run through Yosemite National Park, the Merced River and the Tuolumne River.

The tree line stops at about 9,500 feet (2,896 m). Above this elevation, it's very rocky and too cold and snowy for trees to grow.

Ancient Trees

Have you ever seen a 3,000-year-old tree? In Yosemite National Park, giant trees called sequoias (sih-KWOY-uhz) grow in several places. Just the Mariposa Grove alone has about 500 fully grown giant sequoias.

One sequoia, the Grizzly Giant, is close to 2,700 years old and about 100 feet (30 m) around at its base. It's the tallest tree in Yosemite at 209 feet (64 m), though it was once much taller. It was struck by lightning six times during one storm!

Grizzly Giant

Pit Stop

Two other giant sequoia groves in Yosemite have great stands of these huge trees, too—the Tuolumne and Merced Groves.

14

Giant sequoias, like the one shown here, are in the same plant family as the tall coast redwoods found in Redwood National Park, about 9 hours northwest of Yosemite.

Mariposa Grove sequoia

Awesome Waterfalls

Yosemite Falls is one of the world's tallest waterfalls. In fact, it's the tallest in North America! It's made up of three parts—the upper falls, the middle **cascades**, and the lower falls—that add up to 2,425 feet (739 m)! Much of its volume comes from snow melting high in the mountains.

Other waterfalls in the park include Sentinel Falls, which is about 2,000 feet (610 m) high, and Horsetail Fall. Horsetail Fall is known for glowing orange with the sunset in February.

Yosemite upper falls

Pit Stop

The waterfalls' volume is directly tied to how much precipitation there is each year. Precipitation is any rain or snow that falls.

Horsetail Fall looks like it's on fire at sunset for a few weeks each year.

Climbs and Hikes

From the towering Half Dome to Sentinel Rock, the park is an excellent road trip stop for those who love to rock climb. There are climbs that take just a few hours and those that take many days to complete.

There are 800 miles (1,287 km) of hiking trails in the park, too. One of the most traveled parts of the Pacific Crest National Scenic Trail cuts through Yosemite. This trail starts at the border of Canada and ends at Mexico's border! It passes through seven national parks total.

Pit Stop

The tallest mountain in Yosemite National Park is Mount Lyell at 13,114 feet (3,997 m). There are many others that are more than 10,000 feet (3,050 m) tall, too!

From the top of Sentinel Rock, climbers can look out on the beauty of Yosemite Valley.

A Winter Visit

Most people visit Yosemite National Park during the summer. Visiting during the winter can be cold—but there's also a lot to do! From November to March, there's an outdoor ice rink where you can rent ice skates. Park rangers lead people on snowshoe walks, and many people ski and snowboard at Badger Pass.

Yosemite National Park's special landscape makes it a great place to stop on a road trip. Even better—stay a few days and take it all in!

Cathedral Peak and Mount Conness

cross-country skiing

Yosemite's Tallest Peaks

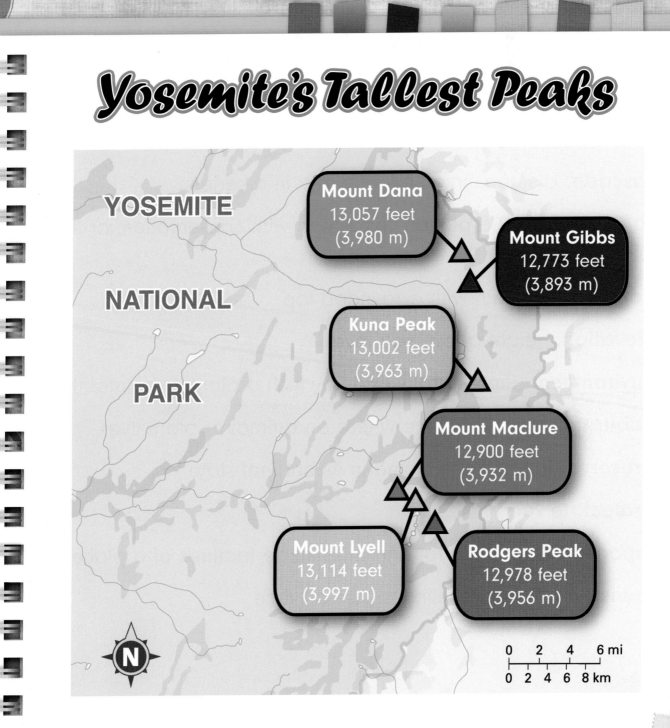

YOSEMITE

NATIONAL

PARK

Mount Dana
13,057 feet
(3,980 m)

Mount Gibbs
12,773 feet
(3,893 m)

Kuna Peak
13,002 feet
(3,963 m)

Mount Maclure
12,900 feet
(3,932 m)

Mount Lyell
13,114 feet
(3,997 m)

Rodgers Peak
12,978 feet
(3,956 m)

N

0 2 4 6 mi

0 2 4 6 8 km

Glossary

cascade: a steep, small fall of water in a series

conservationist: a person concerned with conservation, or the care of nature

dome: a mountain with a rounded top

elevation: height above sea level

environment: the natural world in which a plant or animal lives

habitat: the natural place where an animal or plant lives

preserve: to keep something in its original state

protect: to keep safe

topography: the natural and man-made features of a place

tourist: a person traveling to visit a place

Books

DeFries, Cheryl L. *What Are the 7 Natural Wonders of the United States?* Berkeley Heights, NJ: Enslow Publishers, 2013.

National Geographic Society. *National Geographic Kids National Park Guide U.S.A.: The Most Amazing Sights, Scenes, and Cool Activities from Coast to Coast.* Washington, DC: National Geographic Society, 2012.

Websites

For Kids: Yosemite National Park
www.nps.gov/yose/forkids/index.htm
Find out all the fun activities just for kids at Yosemite National Park.

Yosemite National Park Photos
travel.nationalgeographic.com/travel/national-parks/yosemite-photos/
See more of Yosemite in these beautiful photographs.

Publisher's note to educators and parents: Our editors have carefully reviewed these websites to ensure that they are suitable for students. Many websites change frequently, however, and we cannot guarantee that a site's future contents will continue to meet our high standards of quality and educational value. Be advised that students should be closely supervised whenever they access the Internet.

Index